Retellings

Retellings

Andrew Frolish

ISBN: 978-0-9570984-4-2

Scan QR code for further title information

First published August 2012 by:

Nine Arches Press
Great Central Studios
92 Lower Hillmorton Rd
Rugby
Warwickshire
CV21 3TF

www.ninearchespress.com

Printed in Britain by:

imprintdigital.net
Seychelles Farm,
Upton Pyne,
Exeter
EX5 5HY
www.imprintdigital.net

Retellings

Andrew Frolish

Nine
Arches
Press

Andrew Frolish was born in Sheffield in 1975. After studying politics at Lancaster University, he trained to be a teacher in the Lake District. His poems have been published in a variety of magazines, including *PN Review, Acumen, Envoi, Tears in the Fence, The Interpreter's House, Pulsar, Iota, Orbis* and *The Agenda Broadsheet*. He has received prizes in several competitions and won the Suffolk Poetry Society Crabbe Memorial competition in 2006. A selection of Andrew Frolish's poems appeared in *New Poetries IV,* published by Carcanet, and his poems for children, along with lesson plans for teachers, have been published by Hopscotch. He now lives with his family in Suffolk, where he is a headteacher. *Retellings* (Nine Arches Press, 2012) is his debut collection.

CONTENTS

Part One – Retellings

Part Two – The Wedding Album

Part Three – Testing Boundaries

For Michael, Pamela, Ruth, Edith and Nicola.

Thanks for the stories.

PART ONE

RETELLINGS

FACTORY WOMEN

Remember how the women would leave first,
slipping away like butter from the hot metal
of their plastic-moulding machines.
They moved as one, sensing that the bell
would soon burst through the factory hum,
summoning us to the corner room
to slump silently on the same old tables.

By the time we arrived (the factory men),
our packages would be waiting behind
the sliding glass door of the hot cupboard.

Remember sliding onto the benches
and unwrapping, folding back the crisp
lines of white, grease-proof paper
to reveal our rectangles of toast,
soaked through with liquid butter
and browned like oiled holiday skin.
Summer melted outside; left us in.

TRANSIENT WORKER

The way he used to lean on the machine,
bare elbow on its hot, metal skin —
I always felt that when he went away,
he would leave something of himself behind.
Local radio was neglected
while we listened to his mixtapes,
singing along in the factory din.
And when they told him to get on
with his work, sometimes he did.

At the next machine, I wore gloves
to handle the hot tools
and to purge the near-liquid plastic
but his hands would rest
on the humming metal, not melting
or blistering, and still they were
the hands and fingers of a pianist.

One day he didn't show. And the next.
I kept expecting him to swagger in,
a grin, a nod and an unlikely story.
We made do, filled in, started on time
and queued to clock out in an orderly fashion.
After a week we tuned the radio back in.

Mechanism

He's in there now, shuffling amongst the machines,
inspecting gauges and adjusting motors,
fingertips on steel flanks, absorbing the purr
and sensing rotations, minute shifts, erring whirs.

The cavity wall between us is hollow,
like the cupping of hands to hold water or amplify his voice,
the breath of winter and the early morning
before the light runs into the mixture, diluting the silence.

And in this hollow, the grating of each device
grows into the thumping of his heart, a mechanical clock
marking these moments, a barometer, measuring pressure
and collecting data for analysis later.

It is a reminder, this laboratory, industrial museum,
that I do not have his touch, his way with his hands.
With coal-fire eyes, hard fingers like tongs and tools
of manufacture, he forges new elements, objects in time.

My pen rests guiltily in a shaft of amber light working its way
from one side of the desk to the other, not fashioning
or producing, a work-shy thing: it only works if I make it.
Because of this, something rises in him, in me it sinks.

The land wakes with him, these dawn mornings,
and the machines give way to the grating of ravens,
the scratching of life in the undergrowth,
between the cracked greenhouse and the lip of the lawn.

Now, through the half-closed window on the landing,
I can see him oozing from the trunks and boughs
by the low-lying pond. The fruit and nettles lean close in,
urging him to bury the blade of the spade deeper into the cut.

His hands are clods of earth, natural browns
and rough collections of thickened fingers and thumbs,
gnarled bones and lined bark, with veins like fattened worms.
The Earth is made of mechanisms like these.

River Maps

Rivers of grime and oil
map on his hands
the filth canals of the city.

The Don and Sheaf
flow with the subtle scent
of his windowless factory.

Thick fingers on worn hands
still droning with machinery
draw me to him, clasping firmly;

grasping to mould me
in the stench of plastic smouldering,
while sweat is stinging my eyes

and stopping the furtive look
over sorry rooftops
to where I could be.

CONSTRUCTION

All the forces collide in him,
the electro-magnet, the compound heart,
the crucible of manufacturing.
In the blackened whorls of his fingers
are a thousand stains of invention,
blood-spilled remains of oily assembly,
the carved metal of miners' lamps and stamps
of codes and places on his products —
the physical proof of his passing through.
In his hands, my father inspects the shining skin
of a new lamp, testing the spark as he forces the flint.

Beneath his overalls and grease and grime,
he is distinguished by a starched collar and tie.
Now see him, in this windowless place,
hand resting tenderly on a metal plate,
encouraging its hum, its tick, its work rate
with a carefully forged whisper, and they breathe
together, like one great machine, stronger
than the sum of my parts; they mould, make, measure.

In the artificial light, no one sees the cloud rise,
an invisible fog of chemical bile.
And yet he knows it; senses a shift in the atoms
and an interference in the cogs and whirs of creation.
This is a drama of working men. Evacuation.
While we make our way outside, blinded
by handfuls of summer light, he remains
to engineer a healing process, hands on.
Outside, I bask alone in the warmth of a summer

we had forgotten; formed in our absence.
My father follows the piston-punching siren call
while workers wait in the shadow of the factory wall.

And this is how the myth of factory hero
is pieced together, a construction in time
of memorised tools, cogs, pumps and grime;
hands crafting over fists pummelling, a life
spent manufacturing this man; the myth is mine.

DECONSTRUCTION

My father: naked without a tie,
his strength forged amongst
the obsolete machines and tools
of another forgotten time.

First they took his teeth,
wrenched from him
while he slept on white sheets.
Then they took his belief

and left him spitting blood
into screwed-up tissues;
his shoulders bunched up,
reduced and subdued.

Bits of him were discarded
and replaced by wires and tubes,
LED displays and visiting rules.
Dripping bags tied him to the bed.

So finally the machines had him,
regulating his daily intake, his pain.
The tables were turned, turned innards out,
diminishing returns in a bandage of skin.

THE DAY YOU GO

I predict there will be an eclipse
lasting for hours and hours.
At first the birds will be silenced
but under the weight of expectation
this will give way to nervous
twittering and coded gossip.

The bees will give up
and walk, as if unwinged,
back to their quiet hives
while the sunflowers will droop,
casting their eyes to the earth,
looking for their own shadows
(they will never find them).

And people will gaze
into the sky waiting
for something to change,
shrinking as the gloom deepens:
an abyss surrounding
one small ring of light
that could mark the end
of another journey.

CROSS HALVING

At a shallow angle,
I drew the tenon saw towards
me, blew the shavings
to one side in a cloud
of fine, gold dust.
Finding the pencil line,
cutting to the waste side
down to the depth of recess
before removing waste
with a chisel, chopping
into the grain, paring
shavings clean away,
my work half-done.

The other piece
half its thickness,
just the same so the frame,
when joined, would be
as one whole cross.
Then the waste swept
out of sight into the corner.
Snags of skin-streaked blood
along the length of the cross,
snagging my fingerprints
to the surface, tied into
the whorls of wooden knots.
Sandpaper smoothed edges
easier to my touch and the stain —
a deep brown that is darker
before it dries.
The bristles pick out the grain:
blemishes, loops, dividing lines.

In the corner of my mind,
my father is planing some plank
on his workbench, pressing
the sole plate into the fleshy pine,
sleeves rolled to the elbow
wallowing in the usual grime,
somehow still young, varnished,
unweathered, in his prime,
heart half-full,
grinning teeth and tutting
at my technique and how
a simple job should cost
so much of my time.

THE APPLE PEELER

The first attack is swift,
between the raising of the glass
and the sip,
leaving a flap of skin
beneath the eye
bringing to mind
my grandma with a sharp knife
peeling an apple
within an inch of its life
maintaining the cut
all the way around;
spirals of green
falling away
like the blood on his shirt
easing into the fibres
in teardrop stains
allowing the surprise
to do the work.

Her control of the knife
taking none of the white
sliding under the skin
gliding over the bone
revealing the marrow
and bringing the blade
all the way home.

In the porcelain sink
where he washed away his face
there is a teaspoon of blood
instinctively touched
and I wipe it on the front of my jeans
where it will steal its way
into the fabric
putting down roots
and passing on the stain.

Under the Skin

Out of the umber her father emerged
with the wild on a burnt sienna day;
his arms cradled a fox cub.
Its eyes betrayed desperation
but it did not strain or stir because
he knew about animals
she tells me, a quality of stories
in the sure calm of her voice.
The cub was lost in the meadow
where silk grasses clumped together,
slumped against the breath of winter.

The cub's wildness and vigour
slipped away to die in private;
it was civilised and named.
Two years a name followed and bound it,
was whispered in the crackle of
climbing flames.

There were times when she slipped
into night, when the flames were gone.
She would see the fox whimpering
at the window — separated,
the tick of its claws on the pane,
scratching away at the name.
Muscles twitched as a hand passed
forcefully under the inadequate skin —
something else living between sinew,
a parasite, brooding wildness.

Her father knew,
understood the fox and where it would run.
Behind the eyes he saw the silk hairs
and they returned there together
brushed smoothly into the fading wash.
He watched blood seep
into the blonde sky,
breathed no words, smiled,
let the wind take his sigh,
quick, like a gasp.

Something Like Summer

Her pupils dilate as they
sweep across the garden finally.
Once there was a chair there,
where they drank, stared into clear sky
with quiet eyes — only talking if it was right.

The chair left a fingerprint,
a bald patch on the green.
She has watched for too long
to see the autumn. Keep talking,
it might still be summer.

She hears the whisper
of water passing underground,
Earth sweating through its pores.

The last day passes in freeze-frames
punctuated eventually —
not by her breathing —
but by the knocking pain
that shows they're coming

to take her home.

ANNUAL

The wall you made still stands,
marking the boundary between now
and the year you left,
the space between us
and everything else.

Frost spreads thinly,
stretched like pale skin —
coolness and translucence.
This garden remains a calendar
of your labour, a diary of days
you spent sewing,
tending shoots, growing.

Even now, bulbs surfacing,
old fingers touching new seasons.
Remembering becomes my reason.

THE HALFWAY HOUSE

I sense them leaving but don't look
as they lean closer, reducing their voices,
speaking of other people, other times.
Their words scatter down the corridors
like seeds that might grow again later.

Now downstairs waiting
to sign out, smiling at the nurse
without seeing the drift in me,
the tides and currents that pull
me in and out of this halfway house
like slow breaths in a quiet place,
small steps between worlds.

They don't know that I hear them
through this pillow, these white sheets,
the carpets and floors and stairwells,
and I know their plans and dreams,
all the places they still haven't found
while I sink deeper into this mattress,
not signing in.
Not signing out.

FOR BEST

These shoes are the only shoes
still kept in a box.
Wedding shoes: shining black,
unscuffed, uncreased:
a pair of black brittle tensions,
of fine lines for special occasions.
Here they are again,
heavy in my hands.

We saw too many magpies,
each flying alone, bearing the weight
of grim skies on their shining backs

and there, by the stones,
one more magpie stone-
cold dead, eating itself
from the inside out.
Quick in death, slow
in my eye. Becoming
the earth, and the earth
becoming everything
in time.

These shoes are not the only shoes
leaving prints in the soil
banked to the side of the hole.

RETELLINGS

And so the stories stopped,
dried up on her lips, fell away.
Now there is only a quietness
that has drifted over the place.
Those old characters continue
to stare from their portraits,
but now their names aren't spoken
out loud, no pointed fingers
or raised eyebrows, no fist
in the palm of her life.

She never wrote them down,
dramas and set pieces.
Now they only linger
like fragile jewels on her chain,
hanging on the walls of her home,
in her father's crafted frames.
Names and details escape,
filtered from the passageways
of my heart. Her stories
go out with her, out of the door,
whistling down the alleys she walked,
stirring up the autumn leaves.
All I remember is that she told them
and retold them just the same.

PART TWO

THE WEDDING ALBUM

CITY CRAVING

This city is my cigarette
hanging smugly from my lips
several years after I gave up
and just the smell of it
drives my tongue
to dance on chapped lips
with the skin-wet vigour
of promise.

FRISK

Your words frisk me
like a bouncer
searching for trouble
I have stashed away
under my skin —
substances to pull you up,
fold-away weapons
I would use to threaten
once I have you in a corner
or over a barrel.

When your words flick at me,
doubt bleeds out and scabs
and I wonder
what it would be like
to do the dirty
and then hide it
in a concealed pocket,
half-hoping you find it.

BREATHING

The morning taste was acid,
dead skin and old paper,
like the stale attic
where I found the box years ago
(just yesterday).

The light thinned out —
a time of fool's gold leaf —
the vodka flowed on
and the orange receded
until it was neat.

In those hours you came in and out
of the box, taken in and expelled
with my breathing.
Each breath I took
cloaked my throat with dust,
making it even harder to say
the words I avoided in the days
when I breathed easily.

BONES

We return to the clearing night after night
expecting to see that white glow
peel itself off the moon again:
the owl swooping between spiny trees
and the slick currents of polluted clouds.

At night, stooping silently
under low boughs and heavy skies,
the earth comes alive with the crackling
and scratching of prey finding cover,
shivering through pauses in the hunting.

On the third night, we find the owl's perch,
a tree stump, rotting in its coat of fungus.
Pellets litter the dirt below: little furry sacks
of indigestible waste, the undesirable
aspects of lives consumed the previous night.

Poking through the compressed fur,
delicate bones like wooden splinters.
Imagine the retching, coughing, snagging
mouthful of unwanted bitterness
spat in the clearing each night.

Stumbling our way home down unlit paths
where the fingernails of nightened trees
scrape the flesh from our cheeks,
I look at you as the moon slips from your face
and I feel the bones catching in my throat.

LAVENDER MOON

Many nights have flowed through the skies overhead,
brooding floods of black cloud, leaving a stain
of sediment and memory on these walls and tiled peaks.
It is damp with it, soaked deep into the wattle and daub
and the oak floor bending and sagging under the weight.

I rest my hands on the beams, veins
on these walls of pale skin, and feel the life within,
the hum and throb of its heart, still strong
underneath old skin, listen as it breathes in
and know that it has me like a drug.

These rooms inched-in during the years we settled
like dust into the corners and crannies,
fingers shaping easily into fingers of wood and brick,
fist into palm, the house cupping us with love.
But these rooms are bare now and echo with emptiness.

The scent of lavender from your secret garden
slips around the bedroom door, caressing me just once more
between the day before the last and the last;
and I let it sweep over me and drink it in,
a silver silk of moon slides and touches my hand.

We lie together, waiting with the lavender moon
and the flood overhead, unsaying our dream
that the moon will remember us ahead of all the others
and that your lavender will stray into this house
long after our passage through here is over.

MANNING

Though my hood is cast off,
your lure is bitten down, the years
of conditioning, the compulsion is still there.

I have learned to return, to sense your pull
and I find myself flying, low to the ground
for some small morsel.

SMALL BEGINNING

Here: a river rolls to the Orwell,
over the estuary mud flats, into the sea.
After the rains, it swells into muscle,
tensing and flexing on the flatlands,
a flood from source to mouth; a flood
disregarding the boundaries
etched on these plains.

A muddy ditch beside a field of rape
where a damp seeping begins a journey
of subtle progress, inch after inch,
no sign of the surge the rains will make.
It flows, not yet conscious of the only processes
that matter: the confluence of waters,
the erosion of ancient land, the deepening of valleys,
the gentle shifting of the earth. Your first kiss:
Sometimes the birth of significant things
passes unnoticed.

LEFT UNSAID

These secrets hang from us
like fruits; our boughs bend
under the weight of them.
The light that surrounds us
is not wasted on them
as they swell and ripen.

Our secrets go unpicked
while their season passes
silently and unnoticed.
Neither of us taking chances
with temptations such as these,
so we let them fall.

The apple falls close to the tree
where it softens into earth,
leaking quiet toxins
for our roots to absorb,
and channel to our hearts.

I've seen you
in those quiet moments
between breaths,
when all the colours
of the spectrum spill
from your eyes at once,
revealing passion after passion.

Watching you weaken,
and hide these holes in yourself,
I wonder how long it will be
before I can see through
your translucent heart.

MARINE SNOW

Here in the dark zone
other animals wait,
living off the marine snow
that drifts from
richer shallows.

Light, in its absence,
forgets these shadows
of fish and brittle stars,
but continues to be
the giver, the provider.

These consumers waste nothing
of the detritus cascading
from the sun-filled world —
particles and dead cells,
second-hand energy,
solar indirectly.

But rise sometimes
to spawn
in the deadened night,
coats burning
with bio-luminescence,
each one a sun
in its own right.

THE WEDDING ALBUM

Those were significant times —
everyone said so — the truth
of this is recorded on film,
visible in motion, forever stilled,
and in the angle of light in our eyes.

Old ladies paused and turned
while boys climbed onto the wall
and railings that bound the church.
The crackle of conversation was lost
when the camera stole the moments

from the flood of time. The hearts
of those who were passing by stopped
like old watches: minute hands nudging
the hour. They'll be waiting like that
until the fading colours set them apart

from reality. For now the brightness
is undimmed; here we are, arguing about
who is still together and all that changed
while these old pictures only
remain the same.

WHITE BAND

Because it used to be paler, this skin,
used to be a ring of waxy enamel
which was cast off in flakes and dust
when water crept into the gap between
the metal and the finger.

I liked the stripe, a contrast of white
and darkened skin: the skin exposed
next to the skin hidden, a ring always,
even when it was taken away,
light in summer half-light.

And when it was curled into my fist,
like clasping the silk of your milk skin,
it was a small, fluttering heart,
trembling, growing fainter in my arms,
I counted the beats it missed.

This is the crux of the matter:
the brown has bled into the white,
the margin between before and now
has smoothed away, an eroding coast
unable to withstand the tide, the pressure.

Absently, I gather fingers in my palm,
almost thinking of the loss,
not quite noticing the white band
that used to be there, neatly pressed
against the knuckle of my heart.

DNA

Those minutes and fragments,
left out in the cold
to fall through strong winds
and flourish in someone else's soil.
All the dog ends
of conversations
or the rind of laughter
cut off and laid aside
and discarded later.
A night out, then after,
the quiet streets home.
The torn strips of evenings
sitting in the lamplight together,
waiting for something,
saying nothing.

Imagine if you could take these
forgotten shavings of time,
the moments between going and goodbye,
and link them like strands of DNA;
put these seconds together
to assemble a new chance, an old day.
Would they be greater than their sum?
Stark pauses in silence:
just think of all the things
we could have done.

CARROM

The fountain, water's public face,
smoothes pebbles that will never
know the pull of currents and tides
while in the corner, our fathers
play carrom as they always did:
quietly, never winning or losing
for long enough for it to matter,
returning the ceramic disc
to its endless place between
the lines of Heaven and Earth.

Lakeside,
obscured by a screen of trees
we planted when the orchard
was still new and waiting for
first rainfall, first fruit.
Here the water holds secrets
in fattened ripples and
flattening circles — the pebbles
we drop are lost in the swollen
darkness and will never reach
the sunlight on this low beach.

And we do not speak
of unspeakable things,
only watch the pebbles
slip into the shaded lake
and listen to the carrom
pieces colliding in the distance
behind us.

PEELING

We wash our hands
as if to protect our subject from
an unintentional infection.
The heart is still bleeding,
filling the plastic tray with watery redness.

Accuracy is important. This is a test.
With a sharp blade, we slice
through the thick walls
of a pig's heart, identifying chambers
and ventricles, recording our findings
in notes and labelled diagrams.

We work together,
like doctor and nurse, slipping in
and out of our roles with ease.
I am quite unprepared for the moment
when your hand smoothes over mine
while I am holding the knife,
and we cut through the muscle
with one hand; still in time.

We reduce the heart
layer by layer, peeling it away,
revealing the life that was once within.
The friction between our skin
as we work together to find
what is at the heart of it.

ADRIFT

When night came, it was still just a house
with square windows and net curtains,
frosted panels and a hidden back-door key.
Inside, your scent lingered
and I wondered what we had started.

You pulled the anchor and the stars drifted by.
In turn, each of us left the other lashed to the wheel
to navigate alone.

The roof swelled, caught the wind
while ropes snapped and clapped
against the makeshift mast,
swaying hopelessly over the chimney.
Gulls circled and followed for a time
before arcing back into the horizons
we drifted from.

Days came. We marked them
into the deck with a knife
until we realised there would be no search parties.

Unfamiliar countries
rolled by like sea fog, ushered on
by invisible currents.

Dreaming of a desert island;
adrift, you and I.

Paper Cups

The bags and boxes of domestic items
score a line between them.
In still, clean air her voice doesn't carry,
forgotten words wasted.
Taking a sip, he screws up his face,
adding a few more creases
for her to unfold and soften later.

Used-up scraps of people,
bunched and torn, litter the area
gulping caffeine and courage
for their journeys into the daylight outside.
Their thoughts are formless,
easily contained, poured like pulp.

Finished, he tightens his grip
on the paper cup and makes a dense fist,
discarding the silence

and heaving useful objects
they will never use
and cheap furniture
they will never treasure
or pass on
to anyone.

CORNERED

In the cracks and corners,
by the crumbling sea-wall,
the wind is a dog hissing
in a corner, biding its time.

Down here the waiting wait,
sleeping like children,
hibernating until they can see again
the slick currents which they have lost.

The tide digs its nails in,
dragged back
from the sharp rocks protruding
like foaming teeth from the sand.

People escape,
if they can, or fade
into the sea wall, arching
their backs against time and tide.

SKIMMING STONE

I   Skimming

Pellets of rain trapped
between wind currents,
freezing in the air between us.
Rasping pebbles call out
as I stumble to the sea.

I don't believe the sound carries
much further than this moment.
Collar tugged up high,
resting like a pair of hands
ready to enclose my throat.

Oiled like the important parts
of a machine,
stones slippery in my hand.
One by one I throw each
into the sea
and wait for them all
to come back to me.

Stones, too heavy, too round,
disappear between waves close to the shore,
without a sound,
never reaching their target:
hundreds of miles out.

II   *Stones*

Eggshell-fragile,
nervous, urgent,
pebbles shift under me.

When I am close enough
to the sea's frown
at the lip of water,
I squat and run my fingers
over the stones,
getting the measure of them,
interpreting their Braille.

The stones coated
with a skin of glistening colour
in the tide's retreat.

My fingers are a net
casting for the skimming stone.
The rejects clink together
like small change in my pocket.

I hold up possibilities,
checking for imperfections,
testing the weight until one finds me:
a black disc,
thin flatness of paper,
made for this purpose.

It's all in the wrist
my father said,
the technique,
how hard you work it.
It doesn't just happen,
there's no particular trick,
no short cut.

Nobody knew the lengths
we went to or saw the stone
swallowed
and I am quite unprepared
for the loss.

III   *Skimmer*

Drawing back the tide like your bed sheet,
revealing whiteness beneath,
a secret between.
The sea churns around my feet,
leaking in my shoes, a cool wetness.

My first foot into bed, cold with the night,
learning not to touch you, finding a distance
from which to sense whether the current
is tending away or drawing you in,
while the boats tilt and sway your sleep.

A murmur,
and momentarily the fog lifts,
peeling away the time we keep
tucked away in our hearts;
a dream of the sea,
a thought under the pillow,
a chill in the bone.

Looking left,
the shoreline is broken
by a figure skimming stones.

IV   *Knee Deep*

For a moment the pitching arm remained there,
a ship's mast, swaying above the head,
listing and creaking in the wind
and irregular spray.

I watched, knowing this was a private affair,
obscuring myself between sheets
of sea-mist and greyness.

Then she was gone, lurching into the waves,
thrashing at the blind tide, urging it to recede
more quickly.

Up to her knees,
the current swept her under
and seconds clawed their way
back into the day,
one for each step I could take.

She lay beached and shivering,
raw hands flapping
at her mouth.
Her eyes slipping back
to waves stealthing away
with the skimming stone
she couldn't save.

V   *Inland*

With the towel over her shoulders
she might have been you,
wrapped in the duvet
on those cold days.

The mug at her lips is hot enough
to help her or burn her,
clasped in two hands
close to her heart.

A gust shakes the glass
in the panes, a current of thunder
rips the sea from the beach
over the headland out west.
We don't look up.

Her voice in the tide,
rhythmic whispering,
eroding the stillness
we left in this house;
and she notices how her sighs affect
the walls and the windows,
the lamplight and photos:
leaning in closer
to hold her, pull the towel tight around her.

There's no question of need;
the stone skimmed over the sea
left there now between
the despair and the bulk
of the sky's old reasons.

VI   *The Difference*

It seems right to take her hand
and lead her on to a rise
where a spit unwinds before us,
trailing past the margin of the sea,
dredged up by the storm
and rolled over this morning,
a carpet of small pedestrian dreams.

Each stone that I drop into her bag
is flawed in some manner of speaking:
pock marks or whorls,
inconsistencies of shape.
Dirty sand clings to their underbellies
and there's no trace of the qualities
she sought yesterday.

The bag emptied
onto the kitchen table;
each of these stones could be
a piece of our hearts, I tell her.
If we rinse and polish them,
we might see a difference
between stone and a second chance.

VII   *Last Tide*

There go the vitals,
all indications of life:
the flapping of birds' wings
in the heart;
the timing of the pulse
in the neck and wrist,
synchronised with yours;
the steadiness of breathing,
more a habit than a declaration;
the brain, shrunken
to the size of a man's fist.

Leaving my clothes
folded neatly on the pebbles,
I walk in after it
but stop just before the current
drives me under.
The perfect crime
hidden under the folds
and creases of the sea.

This time when the tide pulls out
like spare metres of fabric
rolled back and revealing
rough stone,
I'll let it go.

PART THREE

TESTING BOUNDARIES

WHALESONG

Suspended in silence, waiting for
the faint songs and callings
folded into the creases of the sea,
breathing stalled; a pause in the bubbles
and froth of humanity misplaced.
Lost and found in the wrong element,
light bending incorrectly through translucence
beneath the shifting surface.

We dropped into deepness,
swallowing blueness, buoyant,
accounting for pressure
absently and fading into neutral memory
of years not drowning.

There's a magic in the act
of levitation above the sea bed,
rising and falling with only the drawing in
and exhalation of air from the aqualung,
skirting over coral fans,
great purple bruises widening like sky.

Here the reef is reckless, rising
in steep walls and monuments
to drifting tides and time;
moray hidden in the fissure
and the nurse shark parked up
between the honeycomb
and the bloody crown-of-thorns.

We rise, like heat, like souls,
hands reaching the glass ceiling
and the dry world above;
we're sucking in real air
as if for the first time.

Before breaching the slick surface,
we pause, holding life in our lungs,
heads lowered into the water
and listening again. *Humpbacks*.

They nod and laugh and speak
of nothing else for days.
My nodding hides
a secret silence. I lied, failed.
I could never hear the whales.

HAIL STONES IN TEXAS

I mean this literally: the sky was green.
Green like the moss creeping through our lawn,
algae in the shallow pond by the back door.
Not the green of freshly mown grass,
but something darker, more substantial.

We arrived at the ranch
to deranged and howling dogs,
running between bullets of rain water,
shaking vigorously when they failed.
Overhead, the porch light swung
side to side, throwing our shadows
this way, that.

We howled and danced to the veranda,
soaked and dripping human clouds.
Someone made a fire and we watched
the storm through the open door:
leaves tossed between bobbing trees;
furniture bounced against the workshop;
power lines swayed like drunks.

Sudden brightening layered the sky —
from a churning sea to the depths of her eyes.
And in that instant, the storm tossed a hailstone
the size of a man's fist across the veranda,
into the house, to stop beside the fire;
waiting for the lazy warmth of the coals
to worry the edges of its ice-coat.

That night the bolted door,
almost shaken off its hinges,
stood its ground and kept out
the stones' drumming feverish fingers.
And we danced in the dining room,
holding our partners close,
footsteps drowning out
the hail's punchy persistence.
Her cowboy boots slithered
over the polished floor,
a peel of new lizard skin
as the storm starved and thinned.

ALICE SPRINGS

I   *Dry River*

Small clouds of red dust
billow up around my feet
on the bed of the dry river.

Pause for a photograph
because you do, don't you,
when you've come so far?

There's no spring here,
just a case of mistaken
identity, fortunate timing.

In this heat, almost everything
is deceptive, even you,
still and breathless

and listening to the hum
of desert air, your skin
glistening like the rain

that might make this dusty
crease into a restless turmoil
of motion and river.

Later, I think of us waiting
on the river bed under
the moon; waiting for the flood.

And you: who did not know
what was to come.

ALICE SPRINGS

II   *Hands in the earth*

At night, we lie awake,
parched and rasping
only in whispers,
beginning to contemplate
year after year without
rain and relief from
endless summer.

What if there is
no flood, no surge,
no reason to return
to the red desert dust,
the evaporation
of our red blood?

It's not good enough.
We plunge our hands
deep into the earth,
digging down to
the water-table, a well,
to raise a cupful from the dirt.

Uluru

They say it never rains here,
and you are blessed if you see
the orange dust welcome the storm,
turning slick and slippery
with the weight of it.
The vast sky dissolves,
losing clarity. Too late
for the skeleton tree
begging at its base.

Half the world just to find
its majesty humbled in the rain.
Already, we're planning ahead,
our hearts scatter like the wind
kicking up the red desert in circles.
Black coffee brings the warm lie
to our early-morning eyes.
Our fingers brush and twist together,
hot winds and bushfires.

But as our footsteps brush the desert,
the stone sky suddenly burns
with bright flames, rock orange
grafted onto clouds and wisps
of isolated campfires.
All the desert's promises
are revealed and laid before us.

FLIP-FLOPS

not discarded but placed
on a dusty bulge in the earth,
unworn, unwalked.

Nearby, a red bag sags,
weather-beaten and steadily cracking
under the vast folds of African sky.

Slumped against a curve of stone,
a ragged doll dampened by rain, dried by sun
too often to count the changes
in the weather.

A blood-streaked shirt,
becoming the colour of dirt,
hangs from a skeleton of trees
and flaps while we talk of life moving on.

In the distance, the schoolhouse
rattles the dry air with the cries
of children the tribal bullets missed;
children who left their hearts
on the mounds of earth
where others left their bones.

We pump water from the well
but bring up muck before the water
runs clear enough to drink.

Return to Bird Rock

Beyond Barmouth bridge, weather changed,
sun grazed our necks: pale white; raw red; leather brown.
The breeze stilled, leaving behind the breath
of yesterday's campfire at Dolgellau.

Short gasps, strength slipped from us on slopes
of silent, wind-choked fells. Creased green skin,
our graceless motion and songs, disregarding
the contours of hard climbing ahead.

Convinced we were the first to know these rivers
and ranging hills, our story was written
in the maps we folded away and with the thorns
pushed aside as darkness fell, making secrets

of pathways taken back by the forest.
Bird Rock rose above all, bursting from scorched earth,
a lush marker on tides greater than us. Close,
yet too far to explore. Passing, looking back, it was gone.

Now look at us, you and me, the first to fold up neatly
into small cases in the boot of my car, looking for the place
we never left. The day is twisted out before we find it.

Bird Rock hunches, barely recognisable. Valleys spread
to the far, grey sea. We climb silently amongst the white crystals
scattered on its back, unfolding our maps, marking our return.

MONTREAUX

With everything I know,
your flowers float darkly away
in the lake at the edge of Montreaux.

Dawn has lasted for several hours
touching the nerves of tomorrow —
a place in the foothills of fear.

I release everything I know
as the cold mountains stare
and the light spits over my fingers.

Testing Boundaries

Along this coastline,
this false boundary
between
each thousand years
sees a mile lost to the sea.
The mist that rolls in
hides its progress
but fold it back
like a white sheet
and you will find something more
has been lost
in the moments before dawn.

And in our house
the walls are closer than before,
reaching hand over fist
across the floor,
increasing the pressure
on the vital organs
and the blood in my lips,
ready for the kiss.

The dense air
leaves me heady,
clasping my heart
and asking if what I have lost
is also something gained.
Outside, the sea is churning,
raking over the shore
and leaving nothing the same.

ATMOSPHERES

Looking up, the sun streams
through troughs and pock-marks in the waves
and the bottom of the boat is a solid black shape,
vast underbelly of a whale, covered in barnacles,
scarred by skirmishes with sharks, coral walls.

Still two atmospheres between us:
I resist the urge to lurch upwards,
reaching for you and the physical heat
of the sun spilling down over the reef.

Economic motion, letting the water do the work.
Wires trail in the dark, snaking from my mouth,
channelling life through an unnatural collection
of external organs.

Air sucked slowly in, as if through a straw,
and I ascend, balloon-like, a few beats closer.
All of the Earth's air, gas and water collected together,
balanced on my shoulders and in my heart.

REMNANTS

Briefly, like the last wave
before the next, he imagines
removing his clothing, layer by layer,
morning by evening, beginning by end,
and leaving each item folded neatly
in a small pile of unnecessary names,
and walking out into the restless murk.

Almost invisible from the shore now,
a smudge against the heaving wash,
he could slide down amongst half-remembered
snippets of sound and vision,
leaving no letter to inform us of our loss:
just a small pile of tidy remnants

for those who still believe
in second chances.

METAMORPHOSES

She sleeps on the sofa,
swelling like ripening fruit,
growing into something else.

My hand rests on her secretly
and I wait for the stretched skin
to stir, to break into life.

The fullness of her is startling
like the surface tension
of a bubble not bursting.

Then I'm talking (without warning)
to this pale bagful of aches
that now defines her in new curves.

And you: I know you're listening
and growing with each word
filling your fluid world, ripening too.

Good Friday

Dawn burst across the sky in a stream
of blood and newness, spilling
over the curve of the Orwell Bridge —
and I kept talking of beginnings
as if they happened every day.

You were bunched up and silent,
conscious of every fibre and sinew
and consumed with the closeness
of the red flecks spotting the tiny waves
on the estuary beneath us.

We fizzed into the ward, dreams coming
in small explosions like matches,
and they closed the blinds on the light,
leaving it behind: forever sunrise.
And all the things that led us here —

we washed our hands of them
at the door, scrubbing until
the old layers of skin fell away.

The arrival was sudden and I took
the baby in clean hands,
blood filling the lines and whorls,
painting maps from which to read
our futures.

His skin deepened like a new bruise
while we waited for him to swallow,
to cry out protracted vowels, toppling
over the edge of our own breaths.
My eyes consumed his fragile lines

marking out the boundaries between
you and I. What might have been
inherited, and what might not;
what blood-borrowing could be seen,
and what was hidden in his genes.

OPALS

With raw hands in the spring chill,
we made opals with breath,
blowing bubbles, slick and oily,
into the breeze and smooth sky,
over the fence, out of sight.

Like days spent in this garden,
the bubbles lasted just long enough
for us to wonder at their spectrum
and miss them when they passed on,
popping on sunned surfaces

and on the painted blades of your windmill,
spreading the virtues of all the gemstones,
their hues collected in patterned fossils.

Each moment, carried by winds of love and sorrow,
the way you laughed as we watched them go.

Two Faces

Two faces float behind a window,
milky skin mixed into the drawn curtain lining,
their eyes, drops of grey-blue and downsized,
follow the cars shuffling in line
on other journeys. They are blank: stalled.
Unspoken claustrophobia, a deep silence
in the narrow corridors, between the close walls
and drab rooms in this old terrace.

My fingers patter on the dashboard;
I'm cursing the traffic, watching for rain promised.
Glancing to my right, our eyes meet,
two girls in their new house in a busy street,
a grubby world away from their home.
And just as I rev the engine and roll past,
one of the girls places her hand upon the glass.

WEIGHT OF HOME

On the edge of the playground
(the edge of the world)
he sat among the grey-brown
dust that gathers there.

Hunching under the load
unseen on his shoulders,
he hoisted and then hurled
pebbles as heavy as a whole home.
Mounting numbness slowly
bruised the air around him
as he watched the stones
skid and skate,
invisible to others.

Squalls of children
weathered his crumbling edges
with unconscious gusts. From far away,
sometimes he looked up.

ARTHUR'S SELF-PORTRAIT

Arthur has a desk in the corner
where he will be less troublesome
and he will not see those things
that sometimes trouble him.
Like the clouds, how they move,
and what does that really mean?

His fingers trace black bars of shadow
the length of the desk, giving them shape.
To define them.

He shouts. Like that. Bursts of volume.
One or two shift in their seats
but they do not turn and look.
They are trained in the art of survival
in the modern classroom,
prepared for the unexpected
eruptions each day brings.
We are proud of how well
they have learned not to notice him.

Notice now, how he rarely looks
at the mirror by his side.
The image he creates is a memory
or a wish; a representation, symbol.
Observe the outline of his sketched self
and the use of thick, black lines.
He'll tell you if you ask him.
Those lines are where he ends
and everything else begins.

One Girl's Silence

She said she wouldn't do it,
could not consent to silence
because it was against her religion.
She said that I would use my minute
to pray to Satan (her words).
I used my minute to close my eyes,
bow my head and hunt for the reason why
I must be religious if I am
to respect the dead.

I thought of her shouting away the calm.

After: a minute's conversation
spilled from the other children.
We burst into the classroom
where she sat alone,
head-bowed and silent.

Diorama

On display in every street: manikins
advertising decadence or desperation.

Here is the boy wearing a cap and casual violence,
marking his route beside parked cars
with a key, a swagger and a forgotten, hard heart.

And her: the girl with cartoon breasts
And Benson & Hedges for breakfast, then continuously
    until bed,
when she will be over-friendly with the local men.
Her heart: an empty packet.

Three children, same mother, different fathers, roam
the estate and trouble congregates;
three times before this night disperses like a crowd,
she will deny them, turn her back, slip away.

Five women lined up along the street, turning tricks
and disappearing one by one from this small town;
lost and found like cuttings stashed in the attic.

Smart suit accessorised by a cheap tie, selling
something in an economic circle of boom, bust, bluff,
counting pennies, spending pounds, never enough.

And in the corner of every room, through every window,
televisions parade the flesh and hearts of strangers.
These representations of our lower selves
swell with the hot air that suburban dreams expel.

Our unholy exhibit
lies beyond a toughened glass partition.
The curious stare in, shielding
eyes from their own reflections.

CREMATORIUM

Shouldn't have asked about the tin box
on the shelf behind the leathered desk.
Until then, these were other people
on the edge of things: only form, no substance.

The box rattled and stirred when he tipped it,
a collection of man-made objects
left behind, rejected in the final moments —
the vanity of jewellery, the replacement hip.

The fragments of their passage,
physical proof quietly taken from the ashes,
the stuff that binds us to the Earth,
the leftovers, the bits that did not burn.

THE LAST TO KNOW

Perhaps I can't quite see it,
as if your hand is curled around it,
a guilty little secret on a crumpled note.
It is something that you fold up
and slip away, hoping I don't see
but half-hoping that I do.
Under the tables, it goes
from hand to hand, lap to lap,
until everyone but me has seen it
and covertly passed it back.

I'm the sort who thinks the worse
if the option is presented;
the kind who worries first
before settling into panic.
When you conceal the only things
that I want to know,
you force me to take your hand
and prise the slender fingers apart:
because in your hand,
I think you hold your heart.

HOLKHAM BEACH, NEW YEAR'S DAY

Fingers soaked in red and orange dyes
had streaked the new sky; roughly painted stripes
on the thin, blue-grey skin of winter in remission.
Dusty clouds webbed across the deepening sky,
hanging in drapes, billowing like sails in the wind.

Our pace quickened. Wind kicked up
sand, dampening our eyes.
Mourning the day, gulls moaned and circled.
Sea marked by a glistening line,
fading into nothing in the distance,
light giving way under the pressure.

The sun grew fat and bloated behind us,
blood-gorged on a black outcrop,
pausing before spreading into the night, waiting
generously for us to reach the milky waves.
Knowing this, we jogged the rest of the way,
breathless and together, laughing into the wind,
hearts stilled and stuck on the cusp of the old
and the new, the blunt familiar and the sharpened tool
of restless possibility.

There are photographs in the box under the stairs:
our faces silhouetted and unreadable,
cleansing flames of the gathering sunset behind
and sea captured before us.
Coats flapping like ungainly wings,
backs to the camera, leaning towards the sea,
sand rippling under our feet.
On some stills, our clumsy forward motion is blurred,

dim figures unrecognisable.
Finally, our collars up at the hint
of the new year's first rain, just as cold as the last,
before we found the car and drove home in the dark.

Debut
new poets series

Debut is a brand new series of first collections from up-and-coming poets, published by Nine Arches Press. The series represents a selection of the best new voices from the contemporary poetry landscape and work that excites, challenges and provokes its readers.

Since 2008, Nine Arches Press have published over twenty poetry pamphlets and books, including titles which have won the East Midlands Book Award and been chosen as the Poetry Book Society Pamphlet Choice in 2011. As publishers, they are dedicated to the promotion of poetry by both new and established poets, and the development of a loyal readership for poetry. Find out more about Debut and Nine Arches Press by visiting their website at **www.ninearchespress.com** or by scanning this QR Code:

studio harringman

Studio Harringman is a multi-disiplinary creative studio based in East Sussex. For our clients we serve as a complete creative resource; strategy, design and production. We have over 30 years experience in design, branding and advertising. Our client list includes BBC, Thames Television, Universal Pictures, Home Office, Revlon, Warner Brothers, Fremantle and the Shaftesbury Theatre. Run as a family business, the studio was founded by Gary Harringman in 1999 with James Harringman joining the company in 2009. We believe in a world where anyone can publish, quality will always shine through.

www.studioharringman.com